Food Chains

By the end of this book you will know more about:

- How plants feed.

- Plants as food.

- How animals and plants are suited to their environment.

- How to use keys to identify animals and plants.

- How to represent food chains.

You will:

- Plan and carry out a scientific enquiry.

- Make conclusions and link these to your knowledge.

- Use Fact Files, books, the Internet and CD-ROMs to help you answer questions.

★ Green plants need light in order to grow well.

Task 1 — True or false?

⚡ Sort these children's ideas into two groups, true and false.

⚡ Write down two lists.

⚡ Now make a list of the things you think all green plants need to stay alive and grow.

> Plants only grow when the Sun is out. If it's a cloudy day, they don't grow.

> All plants have to grow in soil.

> Plants must have water to grow.

> Plants must have light to grow strong and healthy.

> There isn't any air on the Moon, but plants would still grow if you gave them water and put them in the light.

> Plants don't mind how hot it gets, but they die if it gets too cold.

Healthy plant growth

★ Look at this photograph of two plants.

★ In groups, decide:

• which plant is healthy

• which is unhealthy.

★ List your group's ideas about how the plant became unhealthy.

★ Now draw a picture of a healthy plant and label it.

★ Write a report on what plants need to be healthy. You could use a computer and include digital images.

Task 3 — Making plants healthy

The unhealthy plant in Task 2 became unhealthy because it was kept in a dark cupboard for about two weeks and was given only water and warmth. It became tall, yellow and straggly.

✦ What would happen if this plant was moved to a light, warm place and given water regularly?
Write down your prediction.

✦ You could test your prediction using an unhealthy plant that has already been kept in a dark place for some time.

✦ How could you measure how well the plant grows in the light? (Clues: think about height, number of leaves and size of leaves.)

✦ Now try it.
Record your observations as a series of labelled pictures.

✦ Design a table to record how much the plant grows. It should include the date you made your measurements and observations, and what you measured and observed.

✦ How could you use some of your results to draw a graph?
Which measurements will you use?
Will you draw a line graph or a bar chart?

✦ Why does the plant grow better in the light than in the dark?

Plants make new plant material using carbon dioxide from the air, water and light.

 ## Task 4

What goes into a plant?

 1

Think about these things:

- Where do plants come from?
- What do they take in?
- Where does their food come from?

✪ Use Task Sheet 1 to make a list of the things that plants take in. Write beside each word how much you think they take in. Write **some** or **a little** or **hardly any** or **lots**.

✪ Write your ideas about where plant food comes from.

 ## Task 5

Van Helmont's experiment

 2

Over the years, many people have wondered what plants are made of. After all, you don't see plants tucking into a plate of fish and chips! Many people think that plants take in a lot of soil or earth.

This task is about a Dutch scientist called Jean-Baptiste Van Helmont, who lived in Holland over 300 years ago. He did an experiment to find out what plants take in.

Imagine that Van Helmont was alive today. This is what he might write.

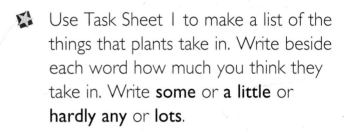

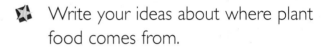

> I wanted to find out what plants are made of. I wanted to find out how much soil goes into a growing tree.
> This is what I did.
> I decided to plant a sapling willow in a big pot of soil. Before I did this, I weighed two things. I weighed the tree. It was 2 kg. I dried the soil, and then I weighed it. The dry soil was 90 kg.
> For the next five years I watered the plant. The only thing I gave it was water. It grew really well.
> After five years I took out the tree. I weighed it again. Now it weighed 76 kg. I dried and weighed the soil again. It weighed 89.95 kg.

At the start

Willow sapling

Willow tree

After 5 years

 ✪ Use this information to answer the questions on Task Sheet 2.

1 Van Helmont found out that plants take in very little from the soil. This makes sense. If trees took in lots of soil there would be a hole in the ground under every tree!

2 Plants are different to animals. Plants do not take in food in the way that we do. Plants do something completely different. This is what plants do in the light.

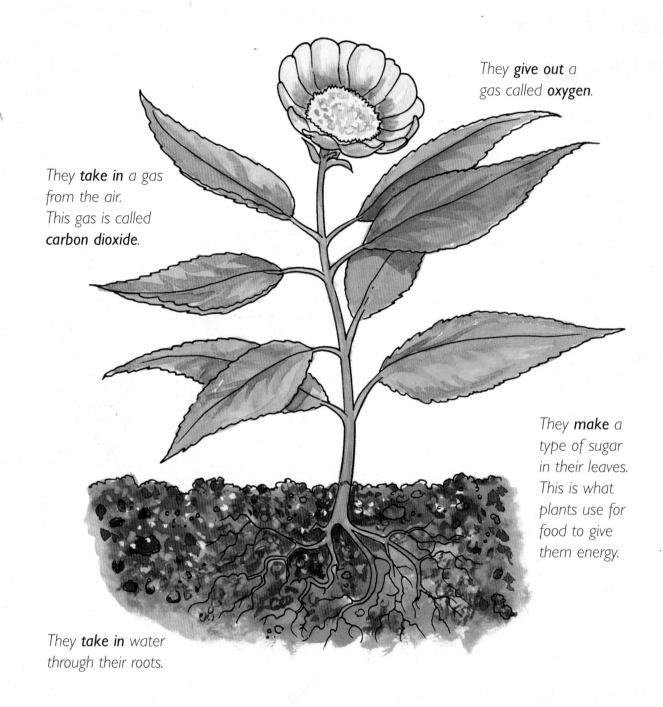

They **give out** a gas called **oxygen**.

They **take in** a gas from the air. This gas is called **carbon dioxide**.

They **make** a type of sugar in their leaves. This is what plants use for food to give them energy.

They **take in** water through their roots.

3 Something special happens inside the plant so that it can change the carbon dioxide and water into sugar and oxygen.

4 Plants can only make food in the light. They use the energy from the sunlight to change the carbon dioxide and the water into sugar and oxygen.

Fact File

Plants are amazing

Humans may be clever but we can't make our food from just water and carbon dioxide.

Plants make their own food. Animals do not. This is why we call plants **producers**. They produce (make) their own food.

Animals eat plants or other animals. Many of the animals we eat depend on plants for their food. This is one reason why plants are so important to us.

Extra Challenge

✪ Do you think all plants need soil to grow?

✪ Try to grow some cress on moist cotton wool.

✪ Many plants grow in soil because it provides chemicals that they need. Use the Internet to research plants that are adapted to growing in water, on walls and on trees.

Words to learn and use:
carbon dioxide
oxygen
producer
sugar

Plants need leaves to make food.

Fact File

More about what plants take in

Close-up photo of a plant leaf

Plants take in many different things to make their food.

Plants take in lots of water through their roots, but they only use a little bit of water to make food. They use the rest in other ways.

The material that plants are made of started out as water and the gas carbon dioxide.

Plants use carbon dioxide from the air to make their food.

Plants have a green pigment called **chlorophyll** that traps energy from the Sun. This energy is needed for making food. Leaves contain lots of chlorophyll and leaves are the 'food factories' of plants. Leaves are the parts of the plants that make food and enable plants to grow.

Close-up of a plant's root

Plant roots take in lots of water

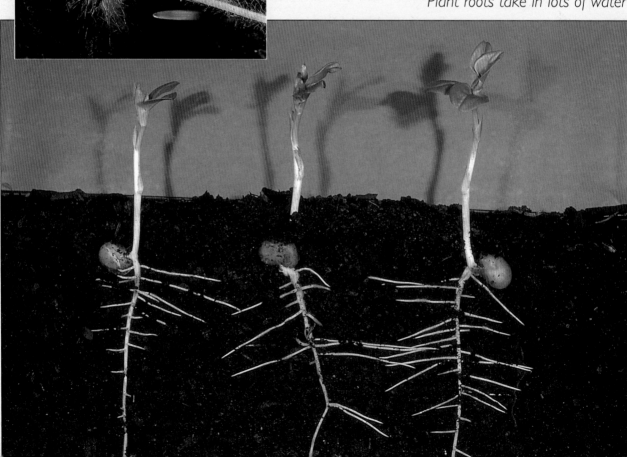

Task 6 A recipe for making plant food

When a plant makes its own food it starts off with raw materials (carbon dioxide and water) and changes them into something new (sugar and oxygen). When we bake a cake we do something similar. Here is a recipe for a cake.

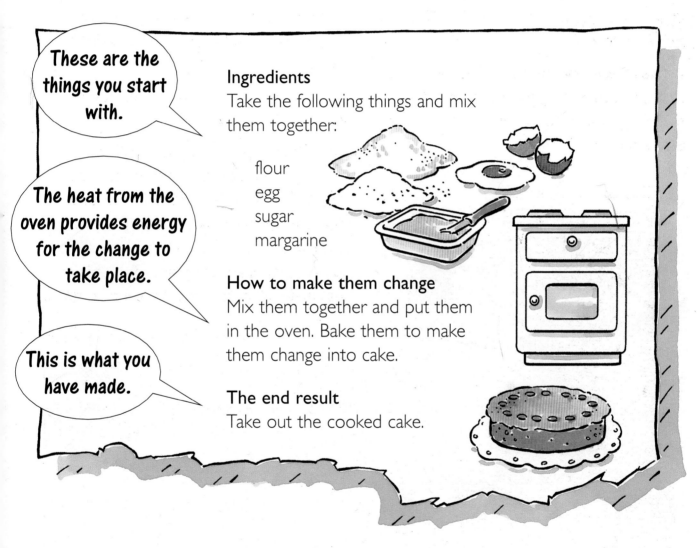

These are the things you start with.

The heat from the oven provides energy for the change to take place.

This is what you have made.

Ingredients
Take the following things and mix them together:

flour
egg
sugar
margarine

How to make them change
Mix them together and put them in the oven. Bake them to make them change into cake.

The end result
Take out the cooked cake.

✪ Design a recipe telling leaves how to make plant food.

● What are the ingredients?

● What is needed to make them change?

● What is the end result?

✪ Complete Task Sheet 3.

Fertilisers are often added to soils to provide plants with nutrients.

Plants and fertilisers

 4

Plants take in tiny amounts of **minerals** or **nutrients** from soil. They enter the plant through its roots.

Sometimes farmers and gardeners use **fertilisers** to provide plants with more nutrients. This helps to keep the plants healthy and makes the plants grow more.

> I'm going to put about 50 kg of fertiliser on my maize this year. I think I'll get a much better crop that way.

> I think I might go for about 20 kg of fertiliser. I don't think there's any point putting more on.

> I'm only going to put about 10 kg on mine. It's too expensive to put more on.

These farmers are talking about how much fertiliser they are going to put on their maize (corn) fields.

Imagine you are asked to advise the farmers about fertilisers.
What would you say to each farmer? Use the information in the graph to help you plan your answer.

Complete Task Sheet 4.

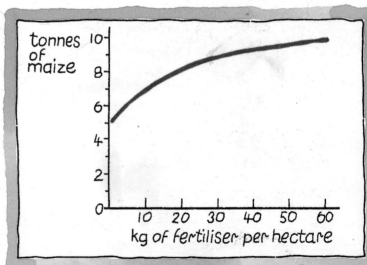

Graph showing how much maize farmers could expect to grow using different amounts of fertiliser.

Fertilisers and house plants

When you buy a house plant, it often has a label giving instructions on how to care for it. The label may show instructions for feeding fertiliser and watering.

✳ Read the instructions on these labels.

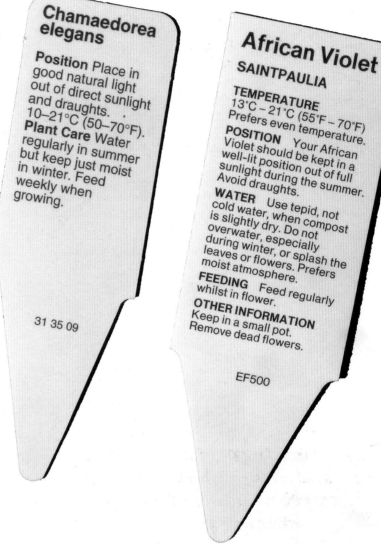

Chamaedorea elegans

Position Place in good natural light out of direct sunlight and draughts. 10–21°C (50–70°F).
Plant Care Water regularly in summer but keep just moist in winter. Feed weekly when growing.

31 35 09

African Violet
SAINTPAULIA

TEMPERATURE
13°C – 21°C (55°F – 70°F)
Prefers even temperature.
POSITION Your African Violet should be kept in a well-lit position out of full sunlight during the summer. Avoid draughts.
WATER Use tepid, not cold water, when compost is slightly dry. Do not overwater, especially during winter, or splash the leaves or flowers. Prefers moist atmosphere.
FEEDING Feed regularly whilst in flower.
OTHER INFORMATION Keep in a small pot. Remove dead flowers.

EF500

⚠ *Always wear gloves to handle plant fertilisers. Do not drink or eat fertiliser.*

✳ Create an imaginary plant and design a label with instructions about how to care for it. You could use a computer. Include:

- name of plant
- where to grow it
- when to water it
- how much fertiliser to give and how often to give it.

✳ Share your design with others.

Fertilisers and house plants

If only they could talk

✦ Imagine that a tree and a fox could talk and that they were having a conversation about the way they get their food. The cartoon suggests how it might start.

✦ Make up a conversation between a fox and a tree. You can finish off this one or start another one of your own.

So fox, you think I've got it easy do you? Well, think again . . .

It's all right for you, tree. You just stand still. I have to chase my food.

Task
10

Habitats revisited

In a previous lesson you may have studied a local habitat.

✦ Talk about:

● what a habitat is

● what a habitat has to provide

● some animals you found in your habitat

● how an animal is suited to live in this habitat.

Words to learn and use:
fertiliser
habitat
minerals
nutrients

Use keys to identify animals and plants.

Plants and animals in a local habitat

Class 6 have revisited a habitat they studied in year 4. They found several invertebrate animals but couldn't remember how to name them. Their teacher gave them some information that they could use to put their animals into groups.

A

B

Use the information in the table below to match each animal to the correct group.

C

Invertebrate group	Special features
Worms	Cylindrical body. Body made of rings, called segments. Wet skin.
Insects	Body made of three parts: head, thorax and abdomen. Three pairs of legs.
Spiders	Body made of two main parts. Four pairs of legs.
Crustaceans	Hard outside shell or skeleton. Feelers on the head (one small pair and one large pair). Pairs of jointed legs.
Centipedes and Millipedes	Long narrow bodies. Head has two feelers (or antennae). Centipedes have one pair of jointed legs on each body segment. Millipedes have two pairs of legs on each body segment.
Molluscs	Soft body includes a head, and a foot which helps them to move. They often have a shell.

D

E

F

To which group does each animal belong? Copy and complete this table.

Animal	Invertebrate group
A	
B	
C	
D	
E	
F	

Naming flowering plants using keys

Keys are used to name living things and there are several different types of keys.

The key in this task asks pairs of questions about the living things you want to identify.

 Look at these pictures of plants that Class 6 found, during one year in their school wildlife area. They recorded some features of their plants and then made a key.

A

B

C

D

E

Plant	Flower	Leaf	Stem
Winter aconite	six pointed yellow petals	like a hand after flowers die	smooth
Lesser celandine	many (more than six) long glossy yellow petals	dark green, heart-shaped	ridged
Creeping buttercup	five heart-shaped yellow petals	saw-like edges	hairy
Poppy	four red petals	divided into leaflets	long and hairy
Snowdrop	three large white outer petals and three inner petals tinged with green	long, pointed, smooth	round and smooth

Identification chart

They used their observations to make a key like this.

1	Is it red or white?	Go to **2**
	Is it yellow?	Go to **3**
2	Has it four red petals and a long, hairy stem?	Poppy
	Has it three outer long pointed petals and three small inner green-tinged petals?	Snowdrop
3	Has it got five petals?	Go to **4**
	Has it got more than five petals?	Go to **5**
4	Has it got five heart-shaped petals and a hairy stem?	Creeping buttercup
5	Has it got six pointed petals and a smooth stem?	Winter aconite
	Has it got more than six petals, heart shaped leaves and a ridged stem?	Lesser celandine

✺ Use the key and identification chart to identify the plants in the pictures.

✺ Write the names of the plants in a table like this.

Plant	Name
A	Lesser celandine
B	
C	
D	
E	

Extra Challenge

✺ Choose some plants from the habitat you studied.

✺ Make a key like Class 6.

Fact File

Where things live

Some animals and plants can live in many different places. For example, a dandelion can live on a lawn, in a garden bed, on a grass verge, even on a road or motorway verge. Plants and animals change so that they can live in an environment.

Earthworms need a moist skin all the time to help them to breathe. They live in cool, moist, soil. They have a long, pointed, cylindrical body that helps them burrow into soil. They have a mouth that is adapted to pulling leaves into soil and for eating the remains of plants.

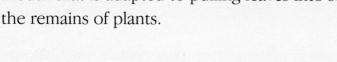
Bluebells growing in a wood

Bluebells and bulbs

Bluebells are woodland plants. During the growing season bluebells make food in their leaves. Food is stored in a new bud underground. The bud swells with food to become a **bulb** full of stored food. When the plant's leaves die, no more food is made, so the bluebell uses its stored food to survive winter.

The bulb can start to grow again in early spring, before the leaves on nearby trees start to open. This means the plant gets plenty of light to make food, before the trees become thick with leaves. So the bluebell grows, flowers, makes seeds and grows a new bulb ready for winter. In this way the bluebell is adapted to grow and flower in early spring. Other plants that grow from bulbs are daffodils, tulips, onions and hyacinths.

How do plants and animals adapt?

✪ Find a plant or animal from your school habitat, for example, a dandelion, a buttercup, a daisy, a hairy bittercress, a worm, a spider, a greenfly or a ladybird.

✪ Use books, CD-ROMs and the Internet to research and design an information card about your animal or plant. It will be used for a school's natural history display or for younger children. You could use a computer to help you with this challenge.

✪ Think about including:

● name of plant or animal

● picture – observe and draw your plant or animal or use a digital photograph, or an image pasted from a CD-ROM

● habitat

● size, shape and colour

● how it feeds

● any special features.

✪ If your plant or animal can be found locally, why not use your information cards to develop your school's web site?

Plants and animals are interdependent.

Task 14 — Plants and animals need each other

5

Class 6 used their information cards to think about how animals and plants depend on each other. They then studied part of a hedgerow and recorded the living things they found or saw. The next step was to label a diagram to show how the plants and animals depended on each other.

The hedgerow

★ Use Task Sheet 5 to draw a flow chart to show how plants and animals in this hedgerow habitat depend on each other.

★ Think about:

● how plants help animals

● what animals need for food and shelter

● how animals may help plants to live and survive.

Food chains can be used to represent feeding relationships in a habitat.

Food chains

A food chain is a way of showing which organisms depend on each other. Food chains nearly always begin with the Sun and a plant.

1 The Sun provides energy for plants to make food.

2 Plants are **producers** of food.

3 An animal that eats a plant is a **herbivore** and a **consumer**.

4 An animal that eats another animal is a **carnivore** and also a consumer.

5 An animal eaten by another animal is called the **prey**.

6 The animal that eats an animal is called a **predator**.

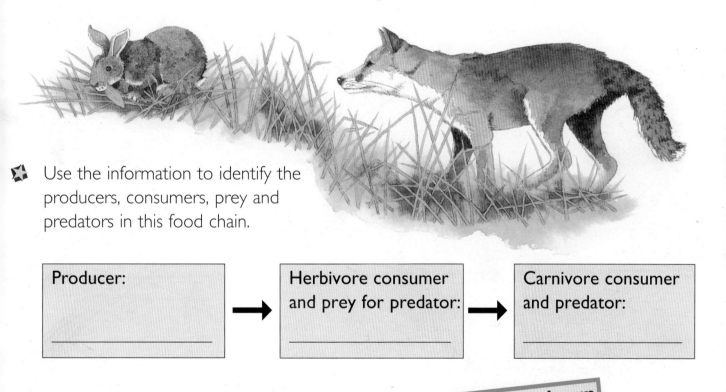

 Use the information to identify the producers, consumers, prey and predators in this food chain.

Producer:		Herbivore consumer and prey for predator:		Carnivore consumer and predator:
_____	→	_____	→	_____

Extra Challenge

 Use all the information cards from Task 13 to help you draw some different food chains for your school habitat.

 What would happen if all the plants in your food chain died? Why?

Words to learn and use:
bulb
carnivore
consumer
herbivore
interdependent
predator
prey

⭐ Different plants grow in different soils.

Plants, soils and roots

Look at the labels and pictures for these two different plants.
Why do you think the soil type is important?

Carrot
Grow in sandy, well-drained soil, in an open light place; water when the soil is dry.

Tomato
Grow in rich compost, in a greenhouse; do not let roots dry out; water well once a day; spray flowers and leaves in hot weather.

Root study

Carefully dig up two weeds – a dandelion and one other weed such as shepherd's purse, bittercress, daisy or buttercup. Try to dig up all the roots.

Put the roots in a bowl of water to wash off the soil.

Look at the washed roots through a magnifier.
Draw what you see.

List the differences between the roots.

Wear plastic gloves when handling plants and soils and always wash your hands afterwards. Do not let soil get into cuts and scratches.

you need:

• two weeds (one must be a dandelion)

• bowl of water

• magnifiying glass

Make observations of soils.
Different animals and plants are found in different habitats.

Scientific Enquiry
Soil types

6

✪ Observe two different soils carefully.
Sketch what you see.

⚠ *Wear plastic gloves when handling plants and soils and always wash your hands afterwards. Do not let soil get into cuts and scratches.*

✪ Complete the table on Task Sheet 6 to show the differences between the two soils. Consider:

• colour

• texture

• size of particles

• dryness

• any evidence of plant or animal material.

✪ Draw and write your answers to these questions:

1 Which of the soils would make a good habitat for a worm or centipede? Why?

2 Which of the soils would make a good habitat for plants that need to anchor themselves in? Why?

you need:

• two different types of soil (sandy, heavy clay or stony)

• hand lens or magnifying glass

• binocular microscope

• plastic Petri dish

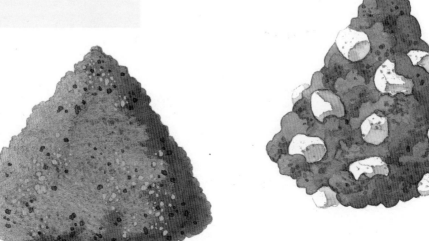

Construct food chains in particular habitats.

Food chains in a pine forest

Pine forest

7

⭐ Research some plants and animals that live in a pine forest. Use CD-ROMs and the Internet to help you. Make some information cards, using Task Sheet 7.

⭐ Create a collage of a pine forest and add your information cards. Use coloured wool to connect the plants and animals into a food chain.

• Which are producers?

• Which are consumers, prey and predators?

⭐ Research a different habitat, such as the seashore. Can you draw a food chain for your chosen habitat?

Checkpoint

Things people say

Look back at some of your work on food chains.

These are some things people say about plants and animals. They are all **wrong**.

✦ Explain why they are incorrect.

✦ Rewrite them so they are correct.

1 Plants use only light to make food.

2 Animals make food and oxygen for their own use.

3 Plants make most of their food in stems and roots.

4 Plants must have lots of fertiliser to make food and to grow.

5 Animals produce food and plants consume food.

6 All food chains should begin with an animal.

7 The prey in a food chain is always a plant.

8 Carrots grow best in a heavy clay soil.

9 Roots take in gases for plants to make into food.

Summary

Which of these do you know and which can you do?

- I know that green plants need light in order to grow well.
- I know that plants make new plant material using carbon dioxide from the air, water and light.
- I know that plants need leaves to make food.
- I know that fertilisers are often added to soils to provide plants with nutrients.
- I can use keys to identify animals and plants.
- I know how animals and plants are suited to their environment.
- I know that plants and animals are interdependent.
- I know that food chains can be used to represent feeding relationships in a habitat.
- I know that different plants grow in different soils.
- I can make observations of soils.
- I know that different animals and plants are found in different habitats.
- I can construct food chains in particular habitats.

Complete your **Science Log** to show how well you know these and how well you can do them. Circle a face for each statement.